INCREASE YOUR PROFIT BY 270%

WITH UV PRINITNG TECHNOLOGY

INCREASE YOUR PROFIT BY 270%

WITH UV PRINITNG TECHNOLOGY

SANJEEV BUDHIRAJA

Available on amazonkindle

Worldwide Published by

Pendown Press
PREMIUM BUSINESS PUBLISHER

PENDOWN PRESS LLP

An ISO 9001 & ISO 14001 Certified Co.,

Regd. Office: 3767A, Kanhaiya Nagar,
Tri Nagar, Delhi-110035
Ph.: 8130886000, 9650072927
E-mail: info@pendownpress.com
Branch Office: 1A/2A, 20, Hari Sadan, Ansari Road,
Daryaganj, New Delhi-110002
Ph.: 011-45794768
Website: PendownPress.com

Edition: 2025
Price: ₹ 349
ISBN: 978-93-7217-305-5

Layout and Cover Designed by Pendown Graphics Team
Printed and Bound in India by Thomson Press India Ltd.

With all my heart I dedicate this book to the business owners who are chasing growth, not just sales.
For every entrepreneur tired of delays, dead stock, and vendor dependence...
May this book give you clarity and confidence to increase your profit.

Sanjeev Budhiraja

Table of Contents

PREFACE

Dear Friend,

I'm not a professional writer. I'm a businessman just like many of you reading this. I've struggled, I've failed, I've taken wrong turns, and I've also seen the joy of building something that works.

This book wasn't planned. It was born out of pain, experience, and a deep desire to save others from the same mistakes I once made. Back then, I had no guide, no one to show me the right path. Every decision was like a gamble. I lost time, I lost money but I never lost the will to find a way that works. And when I did, I wanted to share my expertise to help other entrepreneurs with that knowledge.

This book is written in simple words, the kind I use every day. It's not filled with heavy English or big promises. It's just an honest sharing of my experiences and learnings from my heart. It's for every business owner who wants to increase their profitability and has no clue how to do it. It is also for business owners who want to invest in UV printing technology for the first time.

If you're someone who wants to increase your profit with UV printing technology, you're holding the right book. Not only have I done this in my business, but I have also helped countless people achieve the same. And I am sure by the time you finish this book; you will have a clear path to transform your business with UV printing technology. Let's begin your transformational journey.

Sanjeev Budhiraja

ACKNOWLEDGEMENTS

No journey is ever truly solo. And though this book is written by me, it carries the energy, sacrifices and support of many beautiful souls around me.

To my parents, thank you for instilling in me the values of hard work, integrity, and resilience. Your blessings are the foundation on which every success of mine stands. Whatever I build in life is an extension of what you taught me with your unconditional love.

To my wife, thank you for being my quiet strength, for holding space when the days were long, for believing in me when I was still in a struggling phase.

To my son, your love inspires me more than anything. I believe in your intelligence and vision to create a beautiful life.

To my brother (and his family), who've stood by me in my entrepreneurial journey. You have always been my companion, support and inspiration for your vision and hard work.

And my deepest gratitude for my mentors for shaping my mindset, to my spiritual gurus for lighting my path with guidance, to Pendown Press for helping me publish this book, and to everyone who helped me walk this path.

~ Sanjeev Budhiraja

Who Is This Book For?

Whether you're a newcomer exploring new business opportunities or an established entrepreneur aiming to grow, this book is crafted to add value to your business. It is especially valuable for:

- **Growing Printing Businesses:** Looking to expand their service offerings and explore new revenue streams.
- **Entrepreneurs Starting a Niche Business:** Interested in entering the customised product or UV printing space.
- **Manufacturers:** Wanting to bring UV printing in-house to reduce outsourcing costs and dependency.
- **Customised Product Sellers:** Who are ready to scale their offerings and improve production timelines.
- **E-commerce Startups:** Planning to offer printed products on demand with same-day dispatch capabilities.
- **Resellers:** Looking to expand their catalog by including UV printing machines.
- **Existing UV Machine Owners:** Who need an additional machine or wish to upgrade to the latest model.

What Will You Learn from This Book?

If you're planning to buy a UV printing machine, this book will help you avoid the regret of choosing the wrong one even if you currently know nothing about UV printing technology.

After reading this book, you will learn:

1. **Why Profits Start Dropping in Any Business and How to Fix It?**

- You'll learn about the 3 silent profit killers in your business
- Why customers compare your products only on price with similar products
- Why your margins are shrinking and 4 innovation strategies to fix it

2. **What is UV Printing Technology & How It Helps Increase Your Profit?**

- You'll understand all about UV printing and industries that are using UV printing machines to increase their profit

- You'll learn how to turn blank products into premium items
- Deliver on time, maintain consistent quality, and protect your reputation

3. How to make your products stand out with UV Printing Technology

- Add names, logos, and custom themes
- Print products on order everyday without keeping stock
- Give a premium, fast, and personal experience to every customer

4. How to avoid costly mistakes in buying a UV Printing Machine

- Why buying from the wrong seller can ruin your business
- Which features actually matter while selecting the machine
- What is a UV printer buyer's checklist

Chapter 1

The Story Behind the Book

In 2011, I was running an established zipper manufacturing business in Ludhiana. During one of my business trips to China, I came across printed wooden buttons, a product I had never seen before. That moment sparked an idea:

With limited knowledge, I ordered a flatbed printing machine from a Chinese supplier. The idea was to print custom designs on wooden buttons and offer something new to my garment clients. The machine I ordered had the capability to print on any flat material; it sounded promising.

But the reality was very different.

Two months later, the machine arrived, with no installation instructions. I spent two frustrating weeks trying to set it up, constantly communicating with the supplier in China. Despite the language barrier and time zone difference, I managed to print some samples. I proudly showed them to my clients, promising customised printed buttons for their garments.

Soon, I got my first order from one of the biggest garment manufacturers in Ludhiana and then came the real struggle. After printing some buttons, the printing machine started showing errors. I had no clue how to solve them, and again I was communicating with the supplier in China to solve the problem. Every now and then, there were new issues, and I was solving them over Skype calls with the supplier.

I bought this machine to diversify my zipper business by introducing printed buttons to customers, but most of my time was going into repairing that printing machine. There was a language barrier as well as a time zone difference while communicating with the Chinese supplier. I even found an engineer in India to fix the problems, but that also turned out to be a waste of money.

Somehow, I fulfilled my first order of printed buttons but with a lot of difficulty. Every order has timelines, and I realised that I could not rely on this machine. I stopped promoting printed buttons in the market and was just maintaining the machine. I had invested a lot of money in it, and I knew that I had made the wrong decision.

There was no way to return the machine, so I was just maintaining it. Just to use the machine in some way, I started printing on mobile covers and gifted them to some of my friends. It was a kind of self-boasting, showing the capability of the printing machine that I owned. But after a few months, one of my friends showed me the mobile cover, all the printing had faded away.

I felt even worse about investing in that machine, which was now only good at making me feel guilty about my wrong decision.

The Turning Point

During this time, I came to know about the upgraded flatbed printers with UV ink. I learned that this new machine also had white ink to print on dark surfaces and that the ink never fades. This time, I wanted to buy a machine that was perfect and stable, a machine I could rely on.

I went to China again and visited around 16+ manufacturers, studying the technology thoroughly. After about one week of deep research, I found my perfect supplier and the perfect machine.

In 2012, I imported the flatbed UV printing machine again, the one I chose after a lot of research. This time, the printing results were great. I tested the machine with all kinds of sample printing for 3 months and gained complete confidence in its performance. *I was able to sell a 40-paisa button for Rs 5 to Rs 7 with customised printing matched to the fabric.* I was able to increase my profit easily. Knowing the capability of this machine to print on anything, I was confident in providing this printing solution to various industries in India.

Within 8 months, I helped over 70+ businesses with UV Printing Technology to print on various products. By the end of the same year, I closed my zippers and buttons business to fully focus on providing UV printing solutions across India.

Since then, year after year, I gained deeper insights while working with 1800+ businesses for UV printing solutions. I've seen what works, what fails, and most importantly, what to avoid.

Purpose of This Book

Over the years, I've seen countless people waste their money, time, and opportunity by investing in the wrong UV printing machine. After one bad experience, most of them never invest again and their business dreams get buried forever. The sole purpose of this book is to ensure you don't become one of them.

If you are considering diversifying your business with a UV printing machine, this book will give you the wisdom to choose the right machine for your business.

Apart from this, you will also learn a proven method to stay on top in your industry. This book will show you the root cause of stagnation in any business, and you will discover 4 ways to make your customers line up to buy from you, at your price and on your terms.

Chapter 2

3 Invisible Profit Killers

In 2006, when I ventured into the zipper manufacturing business, I made a bold move. While most players were using manual machines,

That one decision gave me a 3—4X profit edge over the entire market. My margins were high, orders were flowing, and my business grew exponentially for 3 straight years.

But then, the market caught up.

More manufacturers started using automatic machines. Suddenly, I was no longer different. I was just another option. My growth plateaued. My margins shrank. And even though I was working harder than ever, profit was decreasing.

Does this sound familiar?

Have you experienced that moment when your unique edge fades and all that's left is a price war?

The deeper truth is most businesses grow rapidly in the beginning, when they're new, fresh, and different. But eventually, the market catches up. Other sellers start offering the same product, often at lower prices. Your customers no longer see you as special and they just see you as one of the options.

This is not just competition. It's a silent profit killer in your business. *In fact, there are 3 silent profit killers in any business. Let's uncover them one by one.*

Silent Profit Killer #1: Commoditization

What Is Commoditization?

Commoditization is when your product becomes so common, so easily available, that customers compare only by price.

They don't care who made it and they only care about the cheapest option.

Why It's Dangerous:

- Profit margins get squeezed
- Brand identity gets diluted
- You are forced to offer discounts to stay in the game
- Your once loyal customers start asking, "Why are you more expensive?"
- You enter a race to the bottom and no one wins that race

Commoditization is the No. 1 Silent Profit Killer in any business.

It doesn't scream, It creeps.

By the time you notice, your brand is already invisible and you're facing these symptoms:

- Margin compression
- Reduced customer loyalty
- Product homogeneity

- Pressure to offer discounts
- Price-based competition
- Weakened pricing power

Silent Profit Killer #2: The Hidden Cost of Outsourcing Printing

At first, outsourcing feels like a smart move.

You don't need to invest in machines. You can scale without setup. You only pay when you get orders. But here's the reality most business owners don't talk about:

Outsourcing kills speed. It kills consistency. And eventually, it kills customer trust.

Delays become routine: Your vendor says "tomorrow", your client expects "today". Rejections multiply. Colors don't match. Finishes vary. Quality fluctuates. And as a result, you lose money and reputation.

You can't confidently take urgent orders, you can't promise exact timelines, and you definitely can't charge premium prices. The worst part? You're growing their business, not yours.

You're doing the marketing. You're getting the orders. But the profit is split and the control is missing.

Because if you don't own the outcome, you don't own the profit.

Silent Profit Killer #3: Inventory & Dead Stock

"Profit is lost the moment your product starts collecting dust."

This happens when your product has multiple variants in terms of printed designs, and you keep all those variants in ready stock for your customers. But not all designs will be fast-moving.

It is not easy to predict the hot trends in the market, so many of your designs won't move or move too slowly.

Those products will be sitting in your warehouse, your backroom, your office shelves.

And every day they stay unsold, they eat away your: Cash flow, Storage space, Working capital, Peace of mind

Eventually, you start offering discounts not to create demand, but just to recover something.

When this doesn't work, you sell at a loss... or dump the stock altogether. That's not just dead stock. That's dead profit. It usually happens for one simple reason: You do not have an in-house solution for printing on demand, so you end up buying all design variants in advance and keeping inventory for each.

When this three silent profit killers are left unchecked, they slowly eat away your growth, your margins, your peace of mind and ultimately, your confidence as an entrepreneur.

Chapter 3

Blueprint to Multiply Profit in a Competitive Market

In today's crowded and fast-moving market, whatever you create, sooner or later, there will be people selling the same thing. And when your product starts looking like everyone else's, your customer starts comparing you based on only one thing - "*price.*"

If your customers are only comparing you by price...it means your product has become a commodity. And when your product is seen as a commodity, you can no longer control profit in your business.

The only way out is through constant innovation. Constant Innovation is the only way out to de-commoditize your business and increase your profit.

But innovation doesn't mean inventing a new product every week.

It means doing what others aren't.

It means adding value where others are cutting corners.

It means using tools, technology, and creative thinking to deliver a better product, a faster experience, or a more personal outcome.

> "Innovation distinguishes between a leader and a follower." **~Steve Jobs**

The Blueprint to Multiply Your Profit: Innovate in 4 Areas of Your Business

When you **constantly innovate** in these 4 areas, you stop competing on price:

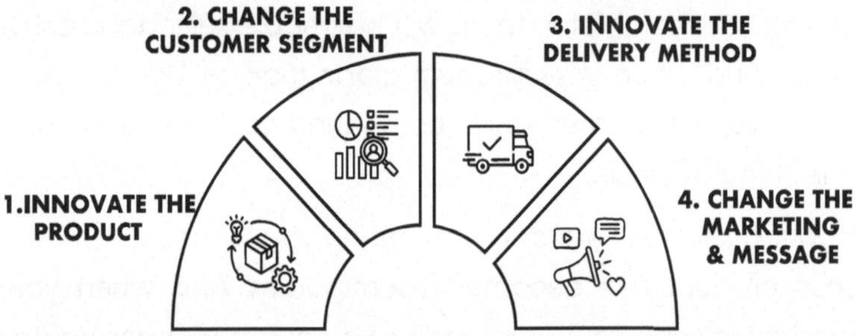

1. Innovate the Product

- Offer a version of the product that others don't.
- Upgrade the product
- Add customization & personalization Options

2. Change the customer segmentation

- Target a new customer segment that values different outcomes, not just price
- Shift from B2C to B2B (or vice versa), from resellers to end users
- Target markets in other geography

3. Innovate the delivery method

- Change how the product is delivered, customized, or packed
- Adopt print-on-demand, subscription methods
- Offer 24-hr dispatch or local pickup options

4. Change the Marketing and Message

- Don't sell features. Sell beliefs, outcomes, and emotions
- Use Stories that shifts the buyer's belief from "price" to "purpose"
- Change the perception of your product in the customer's mind

When you **innovate in these four areas,** price is never the primary factor, even if you're in a common or competitive industry.

Let's look at some real-world examples of businesses that de-commoditized their products through constant innovation:

1. Apple (Consumer Electronics)

Product: Laptops, phones which is a common market

Why iPhone or Mac is not a commodity:

- Constant innovation in design, features, and ecosystem
- Emotional branding: *"Think Different"*
- Premium packaging, retail experience, and product launches
- Creates a tribe, not just customers

Apple fans don't say *"I want a phone."* They say "I want an iPhone."

2. Tesla (Automotive)

Product: Electric cars, which is a highly competitive space

Why Tesla cars are not a commodity:

- Constant innovation (Autopilot, OTA updates, battery tech)
- Direct-to-consumer model (no dealerships)
- Thought-leader positioning: *"We're saving the planet"*
- Customers buy into the mission, not just the machine

Tesla sells vision and speed, not just cars.

3. Starbucks (Coffee)

Product: Coffee which is one of the most commoditized products

Why Starbucks Coffee is not a commodity:

- Personalized drinks, unique names, experience-first model
- Third space concept (not home, not work, Starbucks)
- Emotional appeal: seasonal menus, names on cups, loyalty
- Localized innovation: India-specific items, reusable glass cups

People don't just pay for coffee. They pay for identity + experience.

4. Zomato/Swiggy (Food Delivery)

Product: Food delivery which is logistics-based commodity

Why Zomato Delivery is not a commodity:

- Constant UI/UX upgrades, live tracking
- Loyalty programs, gamification, subscriptions
- Branding via campaigns ("Order Karo, Pet Puja Karo")
- Expanded into groceries, dine-in, and premium club

They don't just deliver food; they deliver delight + convenience.

5. Lenskart (Eyewear)

Product: Glasses which is price-sensitive & easily replicable

Why Lenskart is not a commodity:

- Try-at-home, AR-based fitting, instant replacements
- Smart pricing tiers (₹ 999 to ₹15,000)
- Technology-led trust (eye checkup vans, 3D printing)
- Great customer support = high trust

They changed the delivery method, tech experience, and messaging.

6. Forest Essentials (Luxury Ayurveda)

Product: Soaps, creams which are highly commoditized items

Why Forrest Essentials is not a commodity:

- Heritage-rich storytelling + luxurious packaging
- Small-batch, handmade, ingredient-focused
- Retail stores that feel like a spa
- Premium price justified by experience + storytelling

They turned soap into a luxury self-care ritual.

Final Thought

The market will keep getting crowded. New sellers will keep entering. Prices will always fluctuate.

But if you want to build a long-term, high-margin business,

You need to follow this blueprint: Keep innovating. Keep standing out.

Keep giving people a reason to choose you, even if you charge more.

Chapter 4

Innovation with UV Printing Technology

Your Unfair Advantage in a Crowded, Copycat Market.

If innovation is the antidote to commoditization, then UV printing is your innovation engine. It gives you the power to create, adapt, and respond to market changes faster than anyone else.

The Commoditization Trap

Think of the time when your product was new in the market. You started strong. You had the early mover advantage. Your margins were high. Business was booming. But then the market caught up. Everyone started offering what you do. Now, customers are no longer comparing value, they're comparing price. This is commoditization. And commoditization is the No. 1 Silent Profit Killer in any business.

When the product is common, you have no power.

Customers don't ask: "*Who made it?*"

They just ask: "*What's the lowest price you can offer?*"

You become **invisible, replaceable,** and **discountable.**

My Turning Point: The Birth of an Idea

When I saw printed wooden buttons in China on one of my business trips, my first thought was:

These buttons are so unique, I can sell them in India at my own price and payment terms.

Initially, I considered importing the buttons and selling them to garment manufacturers but then came a second thought:

What if I import multiple designs, and only a few sell while the rest sit in the warehouse collecting dust?

That's when I conceived the game-changing idea: instead of importing printed buttons in many designs, I should import the printing technology itself.

With on-demand printing, I could:

- Create any design instantly
- Avoid dead stock
- Enable constant innovation in design
- Stay relevant and profitable

UV Printing: The Innovation Engine

UV printing can give your business an innovative edge, even if your product is considered a commodity.

It helps you:

- Break free from the trap of sameness
- Offer products that others can't match
- Stand out in a price-sensitive market
- Charge more and earn better margins

What UV Printing Unlocks for You

1. Endless customization & personalization, without setup cost

Print names, logos, photos, themes on-demand, without MOQ or setup cost. Your product becomes theirs. And that's how you earn a premium.

2. Speed in delivery = profitability

- Deliver in 24—48 hours.
- Say YES to urgent orders.
- Say goodbye to job work delays and dependency.
- Speed lets you charge more. It gets you repeat orders and earn faster.

3. On demand = zero waste

You no longer need to guess what will sell. Keep blanks in stock, print only when there's a confirmed order. This means no dead stock, no discounted clearance, and no blocked cash. Your inventory becomes your innovation lab.

4. Premium effects for premium perception

UV printers can do what others can't, white ink on dark surfaces, gloss varnish, texture printing, and raised effects. These are not just features, they're perceived value multipliers. They let you charge more for the same base product, and stand out on shelves or websites instantly.

5. Rapid prototyping & sampling

Want to test a new product, theme, or collection? UV printing lets you create samples in minutes. You can take approvals or feedback from customers and launch confidently without wasting time and money.

6. Versatility: print on almost anything

Glass, wood, metal, acrylic, leather, canvas - UV prints on them all. You can launch new products, limited editions, festive designs, without new inventory or waiting. The market evolves, and you can evolve with it. Instantly.

7. Better branding for you and your clients

Offer B2B clients branded merchandise, personalized gifts, or promotional items that stick around, build recall, and become marketing tools. You don't just sell products. You create assets.

8. You regain control

- No more begging vendors.
- No more worrying about rejections.
- No more dead stock that collects dust in your storeroom.
- You control the machine. The product. The margin. The experience.

9. Cost savings with in-house operations

- Eliminate outsourcing costs and hidden vendor margins.
- Save money on every order by producing internally.

- Gain full control over quality, color consistency, and timelines.
- Use savings to pay EMIs of your UV machine.
- Save the cost of operations of sending goods out for printing.

10. Protecting your designs & brand identity

- Keep your unique artwork, product ideas, and strategies in-house.
- Reduce the risk of imitation or design leaks to competitors.
- Maintain your exclusive positioning in the market.
- Build a brand that customers can't find anywhere else.
- When your ideas stay yours, your value stays premium.

11. Environmental and ethical positioning

- UV printing uses less energy.
- Emits fewer VOCs than traditional methods.
- Reduces waste with on-demand production.
- Position your brand as eco-conscious and future-ready.
- Appeal to sustainability-focused and premium buyers.

12. Rapid sampling & faster product validation

- Instantly print new design samples without waiting for vendor timelines.
- Test multiple versions quickly and get real-time market feedback.

- Reduce product development time from weeks to hours.
- Launch designs that are already validated by your audience.
- Faster sampling = Smarter launches = Higher chances of success

13. Strict quality control & consistency

- Monitor every print yourself to ensure color accuracy and finish
- Reduce rejections, customer complaints, and returns
- Maintain consistent quality across small and large orders
- Build a reputation for reliability and premium craftsmanship

Quality you control = Trust you earn = Repeat business

with UV Printing Technology:

- Resellers can become manufacturers
- Small-town entrepreneurs can scale pan-India with custom products
- Established brands can upgrade from basic to premium

And the best part is you can start with zero technical knowledge. All you need is clarity and courage.

UV Printing Technology gives you:

- The power to say “Yes” to urgent orders
- The power to create products the market hasn’t seen
- The power to control your time, your profit, your brand

And most of all. The power to never be a commodity again. That's the potential you unlock. When you own the UV printing machine.

Industries Growing with UV Printing Machines

Some industries that are harnessing the potential of UV printing to increase their profitability are...

Industry	Industry	Industry	Industry
Gifting Industry	Toy Manufacturers	Glass Industry	Metal Almirah Manufacturers
Signage and Advertising	Food & Beverage Packaging	Perfume Bottles	Silver Coins
Glass Stoves	Ceramics and Tiles	Automotive Components	Consumer Electronics
Textile and Apparel	Furniture Manufacturers	Home Decor	Stationery Production
Corporate Gifting	Sports Equipment Manufacturers	Jewelry	Medical Devices and Equipment
Architectural Glass	Footwear	Musical Instruments Manufacturers	Clock Manufacturers
Luggage and Handbags	Handicrafts	Trophy and Award Manufacturers	Acrylic Wedding Cards
Label Printing (UV DTF)	Banking Cards (Credit/Debit)	ID Cards for Schools & Corporates	Aerospace & Airplane Components

Metal Labels	Trade Show Displays	Office Supplies Production	Wrist Watch & Eyewear Manufacturing
Kitchenware	Flooring and Carpet Design	Wallpaper Production	Bottles & Sippers
Gaming and Casino Equipment	Bicycle and Sports Gear	Digital Device Skins	Hospitality (Hotel Amenities)
Dental Equipment Labeling	Photography (Photo Books and Albums)	Public Transport Branding	Gift Retailing
Art Reproductions	Pet Accessories Branding	Fitness Equipment Manufacturers	Adventure Gear Branding
Travel Accessories	Board Game Manufacturing	Wedding Cards and Boxes	Skincare Product Packaging
Customized Electronics	Custom Doors & Windows	Computer Peripheral Branding	Lenticular Sheets

Chapter 5

Understanding UV Printing Technology

What is UV printing technology?

UV printing is a digital printing process where special UV inks are instantly dried or "cured" using UV (Ultraviolet) light.

As soon as the ink is sprayed onto the surface, a UV lamp follows and cures it instantly. There is no drying time, no smudging, and no delay.

UV Ink forms a molecular bond with the media or the coating on the media, making it durable and long-lasting.

Why it is a breakthrough

- No need for heat or pressure to cure the ink
- Works on almost all surfaces: glass, metal, wood, acrylic, canvas, leather, plastic, and more
- Produces vibrant, scratch-resistant, and water-resistant prints
- Allows printing with white ink, enabling designs on dark or transparent surfaces
- Supports varnish ink for spot UV effects
- Enables gold foiling using specialized spot-varnish printing

- Prints single pieces or large batches without needing to make screens or plates
- Some machines can print on irregular surfaces up to 20mm thickness
- Rotary attachment available in some models for printing on curved/round surfaces (like bottles or pens)

Imagine This:

A printer that works just like your desktop inkjet printer...

But instead of just printing on paper, it can print on:

A mobile cover, A pen, A coaster, A diary, etc

Now imagine that print:

- Dries instantly
- Never smears
- Looks vibrant and premium

That's the power of UV printing.

UV Printing Vs Traditional Printing – A quick comparison

Feature	Traditional Printing	UV Printing
Drying Time	Requires time/heat/air	Instant (UV light cured)
Surfaces Supported	Mostly paper/fabric	Almost all materials (glass, wood, leather, acrylic, etc.)
Print Durability	May fade or scratch	Water-resistant, scratch-resistant, long-lasting
Small Batch Printing	Expensive or slow	Easy, quick, and cost-effective
Special Effects	Limited	3D texture, white ink, spot varnish, gold foiling, gloss effects

How Does UV Printing Work?

Most business owners imagine printing as messy, technical, and hard to manage.But UV printing is surprisingly simple, clean, and efficient.
Here are simple steps to do uv printing on any substrate

Design Creation

You start with a digital design, your customer's logo, a photo, name, quote, or your custom artwork.You can use any standard design software: CorelDRAW, Photoshop, Illustrator, or Canva.

RIP Software Conversion

The design is sent to a RIP (Raster Image Processor) software, which converts the file into a format the printer understands. This software also: Controls color layers, Adds white ink or varnish, Sets the resolution and size

Printing Begin

Once the design is loaded, the UV printer sprays special UV ink onto the surface of your material — whether it's glass, wood, acrylic, or even leather.

Instant Curing with UV Light

As the ink droplets fall on the surface of material, UV LED lights follow immediately behind and cure (dry) the ink instantly using ultraviolet rays.
This means:

- No smudging
- No drying time
- No waiting

You have a vibrant, durable, water-resistant print, ready to use the moment it comes out of the machine.

UV Printing Vs Other Printing Technologies

Here's how UV printing compares to other common printing technologies like Sublimation, Screen Printing and Pad Printing:

Feature / Use Case	UV Printing	Sublimation	Screen Printing	Pad Printing
Materials Supported	Wood, glass, acrylic, leather, plastic, metal (almost all)	Polyester-coated surfaces only	Flat fabrics or surfaces	Small, 3D, curved objects
Drying Time	Instant (UV light cured)	Needs heat pressing	Air/heat dry (slow)	Moderate
MOQ (Min. Quantity)	1 unit (print-on-demand)	1 unit (print-on-demand)	High (one screen per color)	Bulk-friendly
Image Quality	Very high (up to 2880 DPI)	Good	Good for bold solid colors	Moderate
Special Effects	White ink & varnish effects	Not supported	Not supported	Not supported
Surface Types	Flat, curved, rigid, flexible (via DTF too)	Mostly flat or mugs	Flat only	Irregular 3D surfaces
Setup Time	Minimal (plug & print)	Moderate	High (screen setup required)	Moderate
Speed for Custom Orders	Very fast (same-day possible)	Slower due to pre-press	Slow for low volume	Average

Durability	Waterproof, scratch & fade resistant	Decent on coated materials	Good	Fair
Eco-Friendliness	High (no solvents, no waste)	Medium (needs coating, heat)	Low (chemical-heavy, water usage)	Medium

Types of UV Printers

UV printing has evolved into a versatile technology that caters to a wide range of industries and product types. Depending on what you plan to print, the type of surface, the speed you need, and the scale of your operations, different types of UV printers offer different advantages.

Let's understand the major types of UV printers and where each one fits best.

Whether you're a beginner planning your first investment or an established business looking to scale with the right machine, knowing these categories will guide you toward the most profitable choice.

1. UV Flatbed Printer

A printer with a flat surface that allows you to print directly on hard, flat materials such as: Plastic, Wood, Acrylic, Glass, MDF, Metal

These machines are widely used across industries for customization and short-run premium printing. Later in this book, you'll see how different industries are using these machines to personalize and scale their product lines.

2. UV Roll-to-Roll Printer

A UV printer that uses a roll-fed system to print on flexible materials like: Vinyl, Transparent film, PET rolls, Stickers

Ideal for:

- Wallpaper manufacturing
- Signage and banner printing
- Digital painting production
- Footwear lining & packaging industry

This machine is perfect if you work with continuous material rolls and need bulk printing with consistent quality.

3. UV DTF Printer (Direct-to-Film)

A hybrid UV printing technology that prints on adhesive films to create UV stickers.

These stickers can be transferred to nearly any object, such as: Glass bottles, Wooden gifts, Mugs and pens, Perfume bottles, Phone cases

Key Advantages:

- No need to align the product under a printer bed
- Works well on curved, uneven, or small surfaces

Perfect for businesses looking for quick personalization across varied products without the hassle of direct alignment.

4. Hybrid UV Printer

A combination of flatbed and roll-to-roll technology; one machine that can handle both rigid boards and flexible materials.

Suitable for:

- Lightweight sheets like foam boards
- Flexible rolls such as leatherette or synthetic fabric

This is ideal for businesses that want versatility in one machine without having to invest in two separate units.

5. HD-DTF UV Printer

This advanced hybrid UV printing technology prints on a special film, which is then transferred onto fabric.

Allows you to:

- Print high-resolution, multicolor designs
- Create embroidery-like textures and logo effects

Used in the garment industry to print HD logos and branding on clothes without stitching or threads.

6. One Pass UV Printer

A high-speed flatbed UV printer with a conveyor belt system, allowing you to print products at lightning speed.

Ideal for: Industrial production where the same product is printed in large quantities

These machines are widely used in mass production environments, especially where consistency and speed are critical. One pass UV printer is a flatbed UV printer with a conveyor to print products at a lightning speed. Ideal for industrial production of the same kind of products.

7. Rotary UV Printer

A printer designed specifically for cylindrical and round products, such as: Water bottles, Sippers, Tumblers, Stainless steel utensils

With a rotary attachment, this printer rotates the object while printing, allowing for 360-degree design coverage.

8. Label UV Printer

Label UV printers are used to print high-speed labels on materials such as: Transparent film, White stickers, Metalized substrates

Speed: Up to 50 meters per minute

Widely used in: FMCG and beverage industries, Perfume and cosmetic packaging, Industrial labeling and branding

These machines are ideal for businesses requiring high-volume label printing with premium finish.

Common Myths & Misunderstandings

Before most people even step into the world of UV printing, they're already held back, not by facts, but by false beliefs.

Maybe someone told them:

- "It's too complicated."
- "It's only meant for big factories."

- "The maintenance is a nightmare."

These myths stop great businesses from unlocking the real potential of UV printing.

Let's see the most common misunderstandings about the UV printing technology and show you the truth behind them. When you have clarity, you can move forward with clarity and confidence.

Myth #1: "UV Printing is Complicated"

The Truth:

UV printers work just like your regular desktop printer just with far more flexibility.

You simply:

- Load the design
- Load the product
- Press print
- And it's done.

Within 2—3 days of hands-on practice, almost anyone can operate a UV printer confidently.

You don't need a design degree, factory background, or technical team.

All you need is business clarity, a basic understanding of your product, and the willingness to learn.

Myth #2: "It's Only for Large Businesses"

The Truth:

Many small businesses, solopreneurs, and even home-based entrepreneurs are scaling beautifully with compact UV printers today.

- Machines now come in various sizes, speeds and price ranges, starting from under ₹5 lakh.
- You can start small and scale fast, UV printing doesn't require scale, it creates scale by giving you full control over product, timing, and profit.

Whether you are selling gifts, promotional items, fashion accessories, or home decor, UV printing can become your most powerful tool for growth.

Myth #3: "Maintenance is Too Hard"

The Truth:

Daily UV printer maintenance takes just 10—15 minutes. That's it.

Modern machines now come with:

- Auto head-cleaning systems
- Ink level alerts
- Step-by-step guided procedures

Even a beginner can do the daily upkeep easily. A reliable supplier will provide training and support for you or your staff.

If you can manage a smartphone, you can easily manage UV printer maintenance.

It's a simple discipline, not a technical challenge.

Myth #4: "UV Prints Fade or Scratch Easily"

The Truth:

UV prints are known for their high durability and resistance.

- Water-resistant
- Scratch-resistant
- Fade-resistant, even in direct sunlight for years

UV printers use white ink for embossed effects, varnish for protection, and UV curing for long-lasting bonding.

If done right, UV prints outlast sublimation, pad printing, or even screen printing in both finish and lifespan.

What Makes UV Printer a Smart Investment

When it comes to UV printing, most business owners ask:

"How much does a UV printer cost?"

But the smarter question is:

"What will it save, unlock, and earn for my business?"

Because UV printing is not just a machine; it's a profit multiplier, a market differentiator and a value creator. Here's why a UV printer is one of the smartest investments you can make for your business:

1. Ownership = Control = Higher Margins

When you own the UV printing machine:

- You no longer rely on vendors who delay orders, mess up quality, or limit your customization capacity.
- You can confidently say "yes" to urgent orders without second thoughts.
- You gain full control over product timelines, customization, and quality.
- Most importantly, you can charge a premium for better service and faster delivery.

2. Fast ROI (Return on Investment)

- UV printing offers a faster ROI than most other manufacturing machines.
- Many profitable UV-based businesses recover their full investment in just 6 to 12 months.
- In high-demand niches, recovery can happen even sooner, thanks to high margins and low running costs.

3. Premium pricing through personalization

- Personalization is the new luxury.
- With UV printing, you can:
  - Offer name/logo/photo-based personalization on products.
  - Use texture printing, spot UV finish, and even metallic foiling to enhance value perception.

- Customers are willing to pay more when they feel the product is made just for them.

4. Business agility & trend responsiveness

- A new design trend goes viral on Instagram? You can launch it today.
- A corporate client asks for 100 custom diaries? You can start right now.
- A customer needs a single personalized gift for a birthday tomorrow? No problem.

UV printing removes all dependency delays.

You become agile, responsive, and relevant to every market shift.

5. Low waste, lean inventory & high cash flow

- With on-demand printing, you produce only what you sell, no overproduction.
- Keep blank products in stock, and customize only when the order is confirmed.
- This means:
    - No dead stock
    - No blocked capital
    - No clearance sales
    - Healthy cash flow

Your money works for you, not locked in unsold inventory.

6. Versatility = Multi-Niche Business Potential

- One UV machine can print on wood, glass, metal, acrylic, leather, plastic, canvas, and more.
- This opens doors to:
    - New product lines
    - New industries
    - Seasonal collections
    - Customized B2B orders
    - Retail and wholesale opportunities

Whether you're targeting gifting, decor, fashion, or corporate, one machine serves all.

7. Customer retention & brand loyalty

- UV printing gives you the power to say yes when others say no.
    - Yes to small batches
    - Yes to urgent deliveries
    - Yes to custom branding

That consistency builds trust, repeat business and brand loyalty.

When customers experience your speed, your precision, and your personal touch they come back not just for the product but for the experience.

If you choose the right machine, and the right strategy; this one decision can change the trajectory of your business.

Chapter 6

Decoding UV Inks

UV Inks were first discovered and used in the cosmetic industry specifically in nail paints, which dry instantly under UV light. Over time, this same technology evolved and entered the digital printing industry, opening the door to a completely new way of printing.

Unlike traditional inks, UV ink is engineered to do what others can't. It prints on glass, metal, wood, leather, plastic, acrylic, ceramic, tiles and more, offering unmatched vibrancy, durability, and instant drying.

What is UV Ink?

UV ink is a special type of ink that instantly cures (solidifies) when exposed to UV (ultraviolet) light.

Unlike solvent- or water-based inks, which require heat or air drying, UV ink gets cured using UV LED lights. The result?

- No waiting
- No smudging
- No bleeding

This enables flawless printing on nearly any surface, from hard to soft, rigid to flexible. For hard surfaces like glass, metal, or ceramic, a pre-coating layer is required before printing. But for softer materials like ABS, leather, foam board, or plastic, printing can be done directly without any coating.

Types of UV Inks

Ink Type	Purpose / Use	Common Applications
Flexible UV Ink	For bendable surfaces; prevents cracking.	Leather wallets, soft PVC, curved decor, diaries
Hard UV Ink	Designed for rigid surfaces; high durability.	Acrylic boards, wood panels, glass photo frames, metal plaques
Hybrid UV Ink	Designed for both rigid and soft surfaces	Mobile covers, stationery, acrylic frames, gifting items
Thermo Flexible UV Inks	For thermal forming applications	PVC globes, face masks, molded cases, luggage shells

UV Ink Colors

Ink Colors	Purpose/Use	Common Applications
CMYK (Cyan, Magenta, Yellow, Black)	Standard full-color printing; forms the base of all color prints.	Used on any white or light-colored media
White Ink	Printed as base layer on dark or transparent surfaces. Also used for emboss effect.	Glass frames, black MDF, acrylic tags, transparent stickers, PET films
Varnish (Clear Ink)	Adds gloss, branding polish, or spot-UV effect.	Luxury packaging, corporate logos, invitations, emboss effects
Foiling Varnish	Used to apply gold/silver foiling selectively after printing.	Wedding albums, wedding cards, premium gift packaging
Primer Ink	Improves adhesion on difficult surfaces like metal or glass.	Glass bottles, coated metals, ceramics
Fluorescent Ink	Glows under UV light for party or novelty use.	Event props, glow-based branding, kids' novelty items
Light Colors (Lc, Lm, Ly, Lk)	Enhances skin tone accuracy, especially in portraits.	Personalized gifts, high-quality photo prints
Special Colors (Red, Gray, Orange)	For special effects or advanced color fidelity	Luxury, niche, or distinguished branding
Invisible UV Ink	Security printing, only visible under UV light	Currency, certificates, high-security products

How Much Ink Is Used Per Sq. Ft.?

- **Color Inks (CMYK):** 1 litre of CMYK ink covers 700 to 900 sq. ft.
- **White & Varnish Inks:** 1 litre covers 100 to 300 sq. ft., depending on layer thickness

(Layer thickness can be adjusted using your RIP software.)

You can calculate the exact ink cost per design using the preview estimation in RIP software before printing.

Ink Storage & Care Tips

- Store UV inks in a cool, dry place, away from direct sunlight
- Shake bottles gently before refilling to maintain ink consistency
- Use opened inks within 6 months for best performance
- Keep waste ink bottle and head cleaning fluid ready for daily care
- Spend a few minutes daily on basic cleaning to extend print head life and ensure print quality

With the right UV ink knowledge, you're no longer guessing. You're building. Understanding ink types and usage is key to unlocking maximum value from your UV printer.

Chapter 7

How to Choose a Machine That Pays You Back

As I've already shared, I made the mistake of buying the wrong machine once. It not only burned my hard-earned money, but also cost me a full year, a year of missed opportunities, lost clients and mental stress.

But when I finally chose the right UV printer, everything changed. It became my profit multiplier. Helping you avoid my mistake and choose the right machine from Day 1 is the core purpose of this book.

The Right Machine ≠ The Cheapest One

Most people ask, "What machine fits my budget?"

The smarter question is, "What machine fits my strategy and goals?" Because the right machine is not the one that just fits your wallet; it's the one that helps you:

- Solve your specific business problem
- Unlock customization or faster delivery
- Multiply your margins and market reach

You've Seen What UV Printing Can Do... Now Comes the BIG Decision

Which printer is right for *you?*

A wrong machine will	The right machine will
Waste your time	Pay for itself
Block your capital	Scale with you
Limit your business potential	Become a tool of wealth and branding

To choose the right UV printer, you don't need to know technical jargon.

You just need to understand these 7 key features that directly impact your business, print quality, and profitability.

7 Key features to understand before you buy a UV Printer

1. Print Size of Flatbed UV Printer

Size	Description	Who Uses It
Small Format	A4, A3, 40×60 cm, 60×90 cm	Tabletop models, use Epson heads. Ideal for retailers, online sellers, and small-scale businesses
Medium Format	90×90 cm, 1×1.5 meter	Suitable for photo labs, entry-level manufacturers. Uses Epson or Ricoh heads
Large Format	2.5×1.3 meter, 2×3 meter	Used in signage, furniture, interiors. For mass production and big jobs

Don't go big blindly. Choose based on your product size and volume needs.

2. Printhead Type

Printheads are the engine of your printer. They affect both print speed and print quality.

- **Epson:** Affordable, best for high-resolution needs, great for startups
- **Ricoh:** Industrial-grade, fast, durable, good for large batches
- **Others:** Kyocera, Konica Minolta, Toshiba (used in specialized/large setups)

Tip: If you're just starting, go with Epson. If you're scaling fast or need speed, choose Ricoh.

3. Ink System: CMYK + White + Varnish (Optional Add-ons)

- **CMYK:** Standard 4-color print
- **White Ink:** Print on dark/transparent surfaces, create embossed textures
- **Varnish:** Gloss/spot-UV effect; gives premium branding feel
- **Lc + Lm:** Light Cyan & Magenta improve skin tones
- **Special Colors:** Red, Gray, Orange, etc., for niche output
- **Foiling + Primer + Fluorescent Inks** (if needed)

Choose a machine that supports your required ink capabilities. Don't overpay for features you won't use.

4. Resolution (DPI: Dots Per Inch)

- Higher DPI = Sharper prints = Slower speed
- Standard: 720, 1440, 2880 DPI

If you're into photo gifts or high-end logos, go for 1440 DPI or higher. If speed matters more than detailing, balance DPI accordingly.

5. Vacuum Bed & Height Adjustment

- Vacuum Bed holds products in place, essential for stability
- Height Adjustment allows printing on thicker objects
    - Standard machines allow 8cm thickness
    - Some offer 20—35cm for large items
    - Large format machines can be customized even further

6. RIP Software Compatibility

The RIP (Raster Image Processor) is the brain of your printer. It:

- Converts design into printable layers
- Controls color depth, white ink layers, varnish application
- Helps with ink efficiency and final output quality

Top RIPs: PhotoPrint, FlexiPrint, Maintop, Caldera, ColorGate

Always ask for a live demo before buying to test preview, control, and ease of use.

7. Maintenance & User-Friendliness

You or your staff will use this machine **every day.**

Check:

- Does it have auto-head cleaning?
- Is the waste tank easy to clean?
- Are ink levels and errors displayed clearly?
- Do they provide training, remote support, and onsite visits?

Poor support = high downtime = customer loss.

UV Printer Buyer's Checklist

Key Feature	Why It Matters	What to Check Before Buying
Print Size	Determines what size of products you can print. Bigger isn't always better.	Measure your largest product. Confirm the machine can handle it comfortably.
Printhead Type	Controls speed, print quality, and durability.	Ask which head model is included. Research its speed, lifespan, and replacement cost.
Ink System (CMYK + White + Varnish) + Special Colors	Enables printing on dark/transparent surfaces. Varnish adds premium texture.	Ensure the machine supports the full range of colors according to your purpose
Resolution (DPI)	Higher DPI = better detail, but slower output.	Ask for test prints. Balance quality with required speed.

Vacuum Bed & Height Adjustment	Keeps products stable and allows thick material printing.	Ask about max height and suction strength.
RIP Software Compatibility	Controls layering, color strength, ink efficiency.	See a live demo. Make sure it allows control over white/ varnish layers and provides output previews.
Maintenance & User-Friendliness	Affects daily uptime and ease of use for your team.	Ask about cleaning steps, auto-head cleaning, and if training & onsite support is available.

Final Thought

Don't buy a machine to "start UV printing." Buy a machine that will help your business grow profitably, reliably, and creatively. *A machine that makes money every day, not just looks good on the brochure.*

Chapter 8

Choose The Fit Partner to Multiply Your Pro-Fit

You can only generate Pro-Fit when you are backed up by a Fit Partner.

You've already read about how I bought my first printing machine back in 2011, a wrong machine from a wrong supplier. I didn't just lose money; I lost a whole year of time, trust, and opportunities.

But everything changed in 2012. I decided to research deeply about UV printing technology and its suppliers. That year, I bought the right machine from the right partner and the results were immediate. Not only did I make my own business profitable, but within just 8 months, I was confidently supplying UV printing solutions to over 70+ businesses.

Today, in 2025, **Axis Enterprises** stands as one of the biggest supplier of UV Flatbed printing machines in India, with a pan-India service network and the trust of thousands of customers.

The Machine is Only Half the Story

Choosing the right machine is only half the game. The other half and the more crucial part is the partner you choose.

That's what decides whether you grow with confidence or struggle in silence. Most people spend weeks comparing: Resolution, Print speed, Head type, Machine price But they completely ignore the most important factor. The company you're buying from will be your partner for the next 5 to 15 years.

Let that sink in.

Your UV printer is not a short-term gadget; it's a long-term business asset. And like in any long-term relationship, what matters is not the deal you get at purchase, but the support, trust, and reliability you receive afterwards.

Why This One Decision Changes Everything

When you buy a UV printer, you're not just buying a machine.

You're also buying.

- A backup team of technical experts
- A commitment to post-sales support
- A supply chain for spare parts and inks
- A safety net for the times when things go wrong

Because in business, things will go wrong.

And what happens next will decide whether you:

- Save the order and your reputation
- Or lose time, clients, and credibility

The Cost of Choosing a Mis-Fit Partner

Choosing a mis-fit partner can silently bleed your business.

Here's what you risk:

- Machine downtime = No revenue for days
- No engineer available = Angry clients waiting
- No ink/spares = Missed deadlines
- Wrong technical advice = Missed growth opportunity
- Cheap parts = Early head failure
- No proper training = Team confusion and waste

Sometimes, the loss from the wrong partner is far greater than the cost of the machine itself.

What to Look for in the Fit Partner

"You're not just buying a machine. You're buying a business relationship."

Choose a partner who:

1. Is technically sound & solution-oriented

- Knows how to guide you based on your business type
- Doesn't just "sell," but helps you succeed
- Can troubleshoot print quality, ink usage, software settings

2. Has a strong, reliable engineer network

- Regional/local engineers who can reach you in 24—48 hours
- Can offer both remote and onsite support

- Helps you solve breakdowns quickly and resume work confidently

3. Keeps common spare parts in stock

- Printheads, dampers, wipers, inks, cleaners, always available
- No 10-day wait for importing spares
- Predictable maintenance = No last-minute panic

4. Provides training & ongoing support

- Initial training + ongoing tips
- Access to expert help via phone, WhatsApp, or video call
- Daily/weekly SOPs for cleaning, maintenance, and performance

5. Has fast access to quality consumables

- Original, compatible inks, films, adhesives, and cleaning solutions
- Delivered fast, always in stock
- No project delays due to consumable shortages

Mis-Fit Partner	Fit Partner
Delays and frequent breakdowns	Consistent output and complete peace of mind
Panic when orders increase	Confidence to say "Yes" to large/ urgent projects
Learning everything by trial and error	Step-by-step support from Day 1
Constant firefighting mode	Proactive growth planning and strategic support

Choosing a Fit Partner isn't a one-time transaction. It's your growth insurance.

A good machine + a great partner = a scalable, stress-free business

Chapter 9

Your Profit Journey Begins Here

You have reached the end of this book, but the real journey begins now. Let's take a moment to recap what you've truly learned from this book...

1. The story behind this book

One wrong decision can cost you time, money and confidence. This book was not born out of theory; it was born from a **real business struggle,** and rebuilt through the right UV printer investment.

What you've read is a roadmap created from first-hand experience.

2. Invisible profit killers

You've identified the silent killers of profitability:

- **Commoditization:** when your product becomes "just another option"
- **Outsourcing:** when you lose control over quality and margins
- **Dead Stock:** inventory that eats cash and clogs your growth

3. Blueprint to multiply profit

You don't grow profit by doing what everyone else is doing.

You grow profit by standing out and you can do that by:

- Innovate the product
- Change the customer segment
- Innovate the delivery method
- Change the marketing and massage

4. Unlocking your potential with UV Printing

With UV Printing, you can:

- Print anything on demand, in small or large quantities
- Launch trending products fast
- Control your quality, your pricing, and your margins

5. Understanding UV Printing Technology

UV printing = instant drying, vivid quality, no limits on surfaces.

It prints on any surface with no minimums.

6. Decoding UV Inks

You now understand the different types of inks:

- Flexible vs Hard vs Hybrid UV inks
- White ink for dark or transparent materials
- Varnish and Foiling for premium, luxury effects

7. Choosing the UV Printer that multiplies your profit

The right printer is not the cheapest; it's the one that fits:

- Your product type
- Your production scale
- And your business goals

You've learned how to choose the right printer based on:

- Bed size
- Printhead type
- RIP software
- Resolution
- Maintenance system

8. Backed Up by a Fit Partner

And most importantly, you've understood the value of a **Fit Partner.**

A partner who gives you:

- Fast service
- Readily available spare parts
- Onsite training
- And real-time support when things go wrong

The Knowledge You Now Hold

What you now have in your hands is the accumulated learning of 13 years of experience in the UV printing industry. This is more than enough to help you make the right decisions, avoid costly mistakes, and take confident steps toward building a high-profit UV business.

Now You Have 2 Choices:

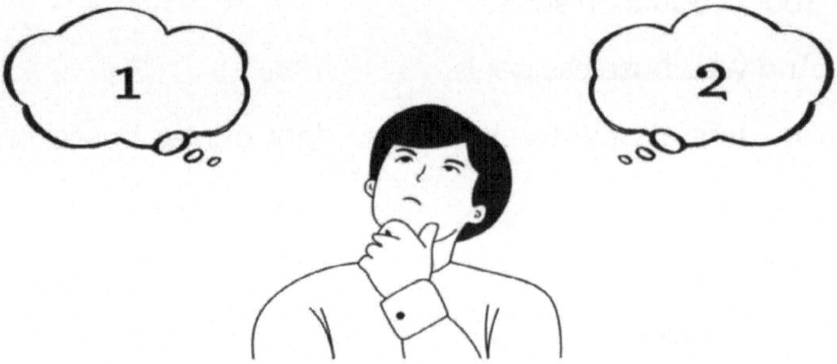

Choice 1 - Go Alone

Yes, you can go alone on this journey.

But here's the truth: **No one builds a scalable, profitable business alone.**

Choice 2 - Walk With Us

You can choose to walk this journey with me and my expert team by your side. We'll support you with the right guidance at every step, till you confidently achieve your goals.

I've been in your shoes, overwhelmed by options, burdened by mistakes, and desperate for clarity. And I also know the power of having the right partner, someone who doesn't just sell machines, but stands beside you, through every print, every issue, and every next step.

So, here's my invitation to you:

Let's talk.

Tell us about your product. Your vision. Your scale. We'll help you select the right machine, run real-time demos, test your designs, and walk with you until your UV business becomes a profit engine.

No pressure. Just precision.

Because your business deserves more than a supplier, it deserves a Fit Partner committed to increasing your profit.

Call or message us at 88721-88721

Visit us for a live demo or 1-to-1 consultation

You can scan the QR code below to connect instantly

A Personal Note to Reader

I've been exactly where you are now.

My journey from startup struggles to building one of India's most trusted names in UV printing began with a personal need, the need to bring back profitability to my own business. Back in 2011, I was manufacturing zippers and facing what most businesses still go through today: shrinking margins and rising competition. That pain pushed me to search for a solution that could bring uniqueness to my products and restore profitability to my business.

That journey led me to UV printing. I bought my first UV machine to print on buttons but I chose the wrong machine and the wrong supplier. I spent one year struggling, wasting time, money, and opportunities.

But I didn't give up.

I did deep research. I understood the technology.

I chose the right machine from the right supplier and I never looked back.

Axis Enterprises: A Brand Built on First-Hand Struggle

Today in 2025, as the Founder of Axis Enterprises, I lead a team of 60+ experts who serve thousands of customers across 51+ industries.

We provide:

- UV printing machines
- Certified consumables
- Spare parts
- End-to-end after-sales support

What sets us apart is that I first implemented this technology in my own business and now, Axis Enterprises has installed more UV printers than anyone else in the country.

We've helped scale UV printing for companies like:

Samsonite, Havells, Emerald, Liberty, IGP.com and FNP many others.

With our pan-India service network, we provide on-site support wherever you are, so your business never stops.

Scan the QR Code and see real video feedback from customers who chose Axis Enterprises as their UV printing partner.

You've Made It This Far, Now It's Time to Act

If you're reading this, you're already ahead of most people.

You now know what others only realize after making costly mistakes.

But let's be honest, reading alone doesn't change your business. Action does.

So if this book gave you clarity...

If your head is buzzing with product ideas...

If you're finally ready to take control of your product quality, pricing, and profit...

Come see the machines live. Get your own samples printed. Ask us anything.

We'll walk you through everything, at your pace.

No pressure. No push.

Just a genuine, transparent conversation to help you move forward with confidence.

Call or Message Us at 88721-88721

For a **1-to-1 consultation** or **live demo**

Let's build something profitable together.

With Warm Regards,

Sanjeev Budhiraja